CW01651972

GCSE Maths (9-1) Higher Practice Exam Papers- Platinum Tier

Specifically designed for the Edexcel exam board

GCSE Maths (9-1) Higher Practice Exam Papers- Platinum Tier comprises a complete exam series for higher tier students together with easy-to-follow mark schemes. Platinum Tier papers are more difficult than past papers, what we describe as level 5 to "level 10". These papers are perfect for students who comfortably achieve a level 9 in past paper exams.

These papers also match the format of an actual Edexcel past paper to simulate the experience of sitting the final exam.

This exam series contains

- non-calculator paper x1

- calculator paper x2

- easy-to-follow mark scheme x3

ISBN 978-1-7391325-3-8

Contents

Paper 1 3

Paper 2 23

Paper 3 40

Paper 1 Mark Scheme 59

Paper 2 Mark Scheme 68

Paper 3 Mark Scheme 77

Surname	
Other Names	
Signature	

The Exam Library

Centre Number	
Candidate Number	

Edexcel Mathematics Higher Platinum Tier

GCSE (9-1)

Paper 1 (Non-Calculator)

1 hour 30 minutes

Total

You may **not** use a calculator for this paper.

Instructions

- Use black ink or ball-point pen.
- Fill in the boxes at the top of this page with your surname, other names, centre number and candidate number.
- Answer the questions in the spaces provided.
- Show sufficient working to make your methods clear. Answers that do not show full working may not be awarded full marks.
- Answers should be given to three significant figures unless otherwise stated.

Advice

- Read each question carefully.
- Check your answers at the end if you have time.
- Try to answer every question.

Information

- There are 19 questions in this paper. The total number of marks for this paper is 80.
- The marks for each question are shown in brackets.
- Platinum tier papers are designed to be more difficult than a normal higher tier paper exam. This paper comprises questions from grade 5 to "grade 10".

Write down all of your working for each question.

1. Work out $\frac{5}{24} - 4.375$

....

(Total for Question 1 is 3 marks)

2. Express 11011 as a product of prime numbers.

....

(Total for Question 2 is 2 marks)

3. Alfonso buys a box of pens for £8.

He repackages the pens into packs of 15.
He sells each pack for £1.50.

He makes 12.5% profit.

Work out how many pens Alfonso sold.

....

(Total for Question 3 is 3 marks)

4. Mary mixes blue, red and yellow paint to make a new colour.

The volume of blue paint to red paint is in the ratio 10:3
The volume of red paint to yellow paint is in the ratio 5:8

She mixes 44.5 litres of paint.

How many litres of yellow paint does she use?

....

(Total for Question 4 is 3 marks)

5. A waste disposal worker has to move 6.38 tonnes of rubbish.

The worker packs the rubbish into boxes that have a volume 489 litres.
The density of rubbish in each box is 55.4 kg/m^3.

a) Estimate how many boxes the worker will use to pack the rubbish.

....

(3)

The waste disposal worker has the opportunity to use a machine to compress the rubbish in each box.

The machine will compress the rubbish in each box to a density of 143 kg/m^3.

b) How does this affect your answer to part (a)?

....

....

....

(1)

(Total for Question 5 is 4 marks)

6. Here is a solid cylinder.

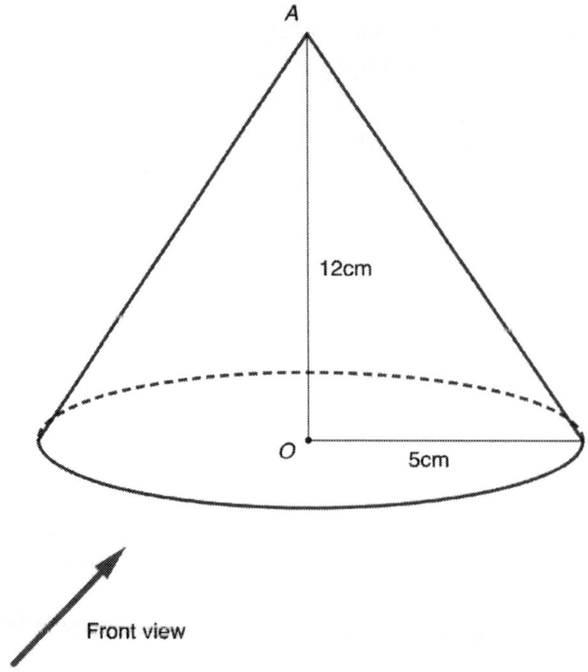

The base of the cylinder is a circle with radius 5 cm.
The height of the cylinder is 12 cm.

a) Draw an accurate front elevation of the cone from the direction of the arrow.

(2)

b) Work out the total surface area of the cone. Give your answer exactly.

....

(4)

(Total for Question 6 is 6 marks)

7. The triangle ABC is equilateral.

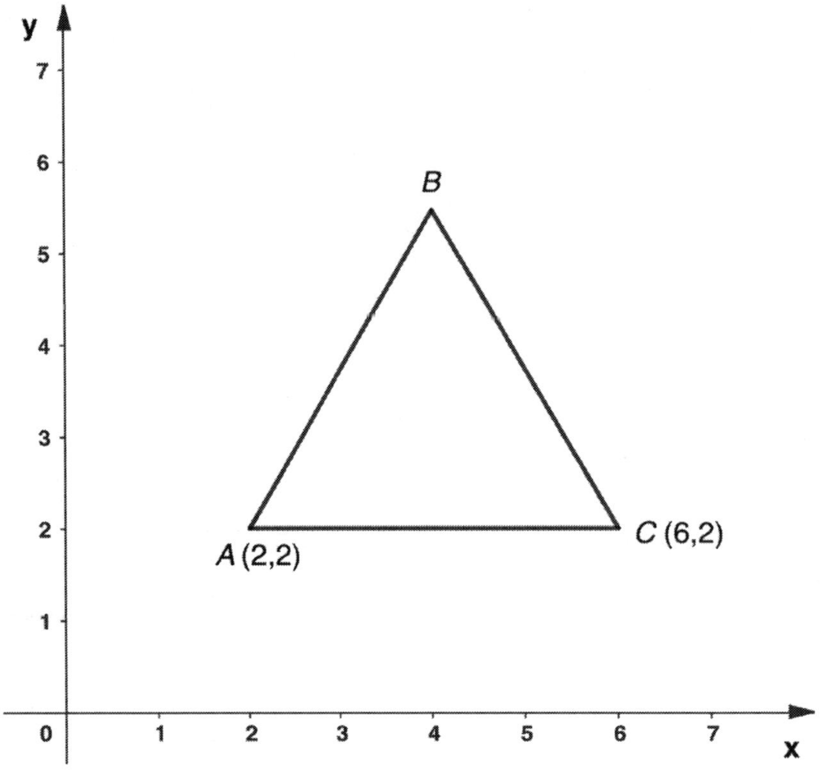

Point A has coordinates (2, 2).
Point C has coordinates (6, 2).

Calculate the exact coordinates of the point B.

....

(Total for Question 7 is 5 marks)

8.

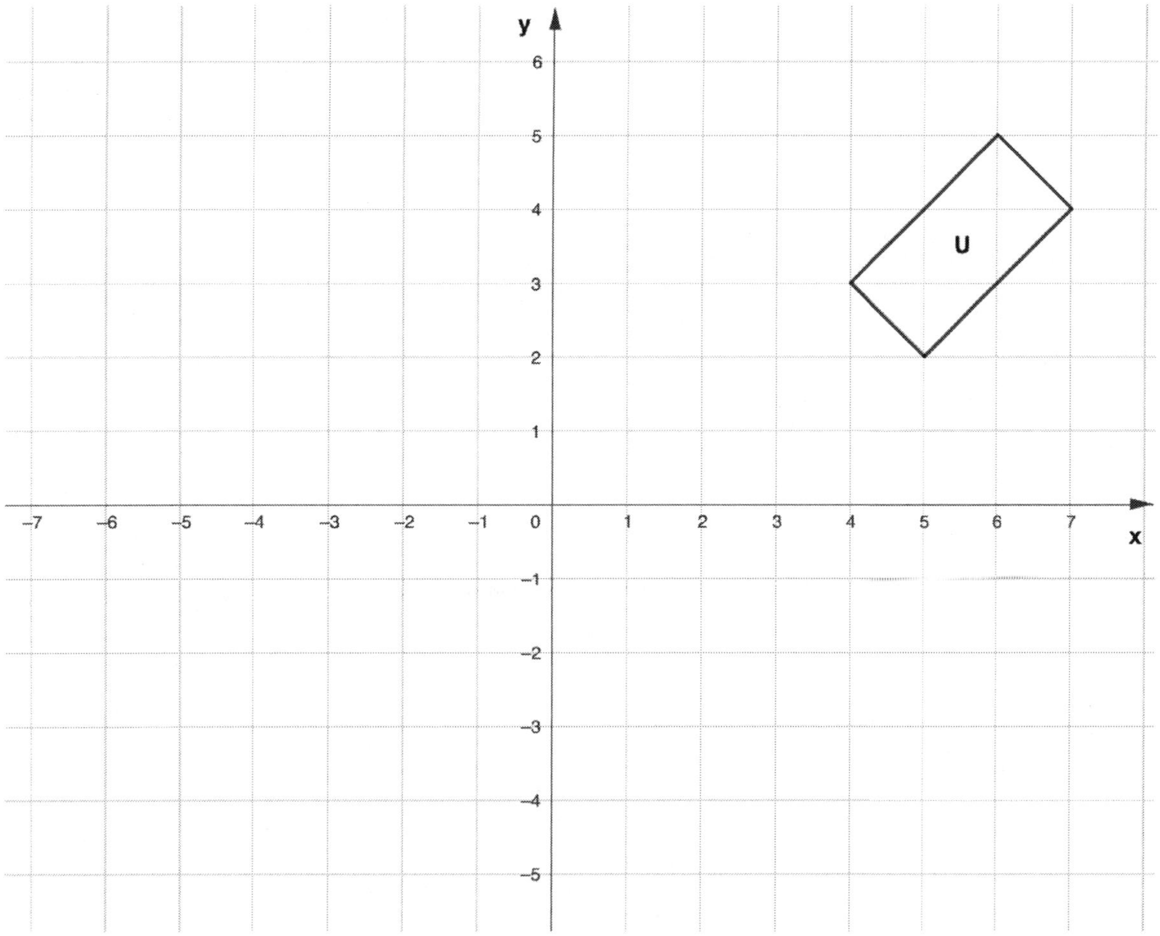

The shape **U** is reflected in the line $y = 1$ to give the shape **V**.
The shape **V** is reflected in the line $y = x - 2$ to give the shape **W**.

Describe the single transformation that will map shape **U** to shape **W**.

(Total for Question 8 is 2 marks)

9.

a) Write down the value of $8^{\frac{1}{3}}$

....
(1)

b) Write down the value of -2^0

....
(1)

c) Work out the value of $27^{-\frac{5}{6}}$. Write your answer in surd form.

....
(4)

(Total for Question 9 is 6 marks)

10. f and g are functions such that

$$f(x) = (x-2)^2, \qquad g(x) = \frac{2}{(x+2)^2}$$

a) Find f(g(0)).

....

(2)

b) Find $f(g(x))$, giving your answer in simplest form.

....

(4)

(Total for Question 10 is 6 marks)

11.

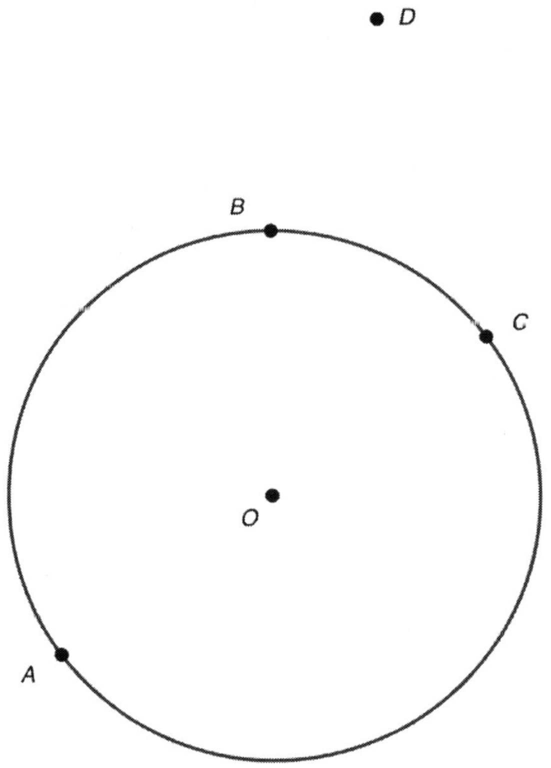

A, *B* and *C* are points on a circle, centre *O*.

D lies on the same straight line as *A* and *B*.
AOC is a straight line.
Angle $BCD = x^\circ$

Find the size of angle *BDC* in terms of *x*.
Give your answer in simplest form.
Give reasons for each stage of your working.

(Total for Question 11 is 5 marks)

12. e is inversely proportional to f^n.

When $e = 8, f = 1$
When $e = 0.5, f = 2$

Find a formula for e in terms of f.
Give your answer in its simplest form.

....

(Total for Question 12 is 5 marks)

13. Show that $\dfrac{9x^2 + 12x}{9x^2 + 6x - 8} - \dfrac{6x + 4}{9x^2 - 4} \equiv a$ and find the value of the integer a.

(Total for Question 13 is 4 marks)

14.

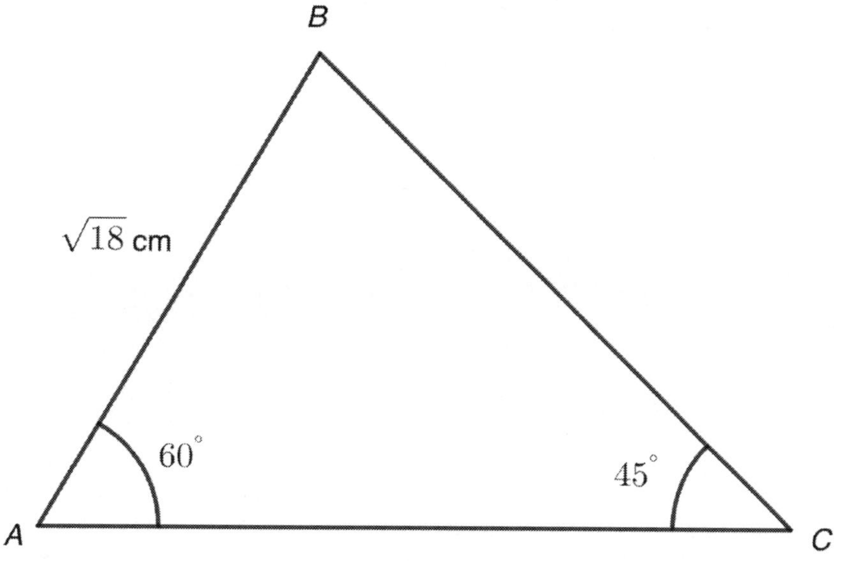

The diagram shows triangle *ABC*.

The side *AB* has length $\sqrt{18}$ cm.
The angle *BAC* is 60°.
The angle *ACB* is 45°.

Find the exact length of the side *BC*.

....

(Total for Question 14 is 5 marks)

15. Prove that every square number is either a multiple of 3 or one more than a multiple of 3.

(Total for Question 15 is 5 marks)

16. The right-angled triangle ABC has coordinates $A(x-2, x)$, $B(7, 5)$ and $C(x+6, x)$.

The side AC is the hypotenuse.

Work out the possible coordinates of the point A.

....

(Total for Question 16 is 5 marks)

17. There are only blue counters and red counters in a bag.
The ratio of blue to red counters is 3: 4

Sally removes a red counter from the bag.

The probability she removes another red counter from the bag is $\frac{5}{9}$

Calculate how many blue counters were originally in the bag.

....

(Total for Question 17 is 4 marks)

18. Sketch the graph $y = 1.5\cos(x + 30)°$ for $-90 \leq x < 360$

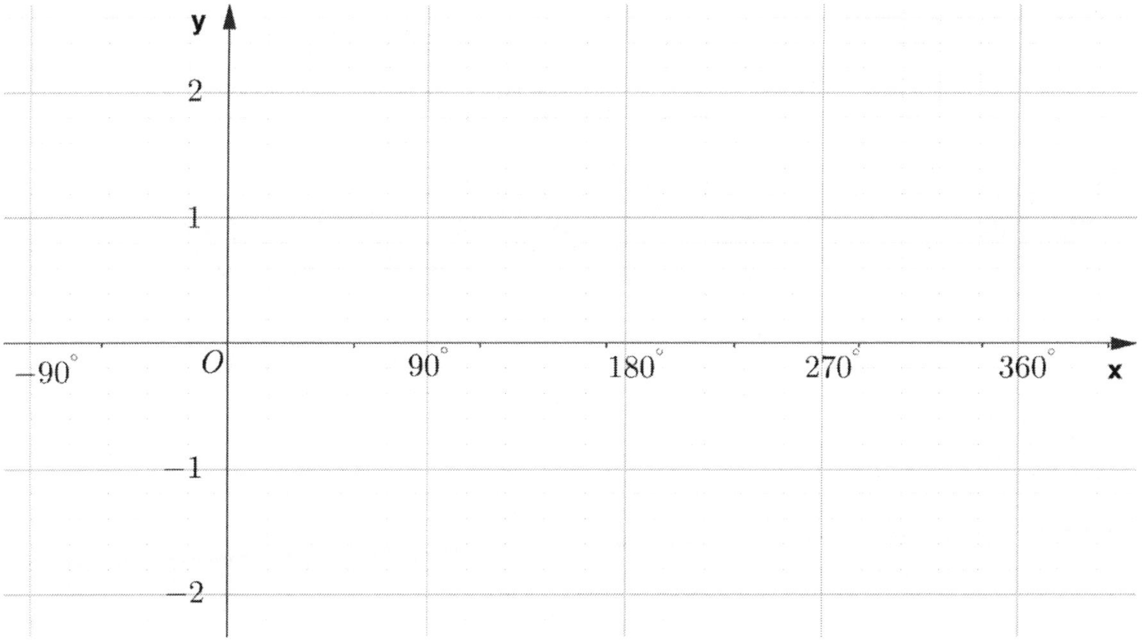

(Total for Question 18 is 3 marks)

19. The equation of the curve C is given by $y = x^2\sqrt{3} + 6x + 19$.

Find the coordinates of the minimum point of the curve.

....

(Total for Question 19 is 4 marks)

TOTAL FOR PAPER IS 80 MARKS

WRITE INSIDE THE
GREY BORDER

Surname	
Other Names	
Signature	

The Exam Library

Centre Number	
Candidate Number	

Edexcel Mathematics Higher Platinum Tier

GCSE (9-1)

Paper 2 (Calculator)

Total

1 hour 30 minutes

You may use a calculator for this paper.

Instructions

- Use black ink or ball-point pen.
- Fill in the boxes at the top of this page with your surname, other names, centre number and candidate number.
- Answer the questions in the spaces provided.
- Show sufficient working to make your methods clear. Answers that do not show full working may not be awarded full marks.
- Answers should be given to three significant figures unless otherwise stated.

Advice

- Read each question carefully.
- Check your answers at the end if you have time.
- Try to answer every question.

Information

- There are 18 questions in this paper. The total number of marks for this paper is 80.
- The marks for each question are shown in brackets.
- Platinum tier papers are designed to be more difficult than a normal higher tier paper exam. This paper comprises questions from grade 5 to "grade 10".

Write down all of your working for each question.

1. Find the highest common factor of 264 and 4356.

....

(Total for Question 1 is 3 marks)

2.

a) Expand and simplify $6a\left(a^2+\frac{x}{a}\right)$

....

(1)

b) Expand and simplify $2x\sqrt{x}(x^{2.5}-2xy+8y)$

....

(2)

c) Expand and simplify $x^{-\frac{3}{2}}(x^2+x^3)+10\sqrt{x}$

....

(2)

(Total for Question 2 is 5 marks)

3. Miguel buys a vintage car.

It appreciates in value by 5% each year over 3 years.

He sells the car at the end of the 3 years.

Find the ratio of the original cost to the profit he makes.

....

(Total for Question 3 is 4 marks)

4. The line $y = -2x + 5$ defined on $0 \leq x \leq 4$ is the diagonal of a rhombus.

a) Find the equation of the second diagonal of the rhombus.

....

(4)

b) Find suitable x values for which the other diagonal is defined.

....

(2)

(Total for Question 4 is 6 marks)

5. Solve $10 - \frac{24}{x} = x$

....

(Total for Question 5 is 3 marks)

6. Selma runs a cross country race.

To beat her personal best, she must run under 40 minutes.

The race is 10,000 m to the nearest 1000 m.

Her average speed is 14 kmh^{-1} to the nearest whole number.

Show Selma could have beaten her personal best.

....

(Total for Question 6 is 4 marks)

7.

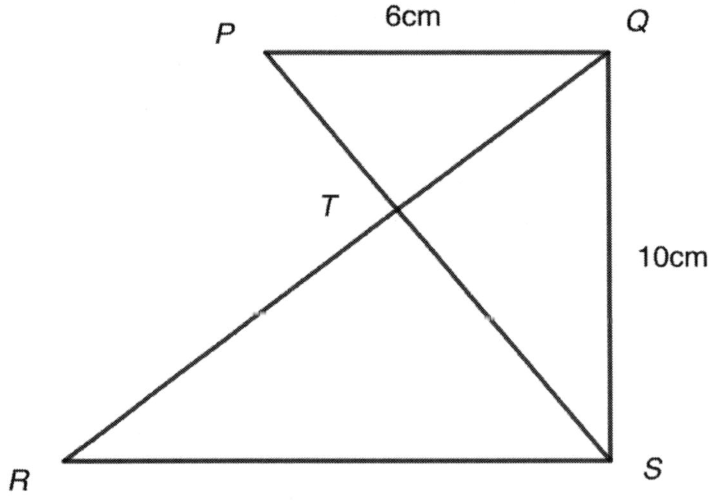

$PQ = 6$ cm
$QS = 10$ cm

Angle PQS = angle QSR = angle $QTS = 90°$

Calculate the size of angle QRS.
Give a reason for each stage of your working.

....

(Total for Question 7 is 5 marks)

8.

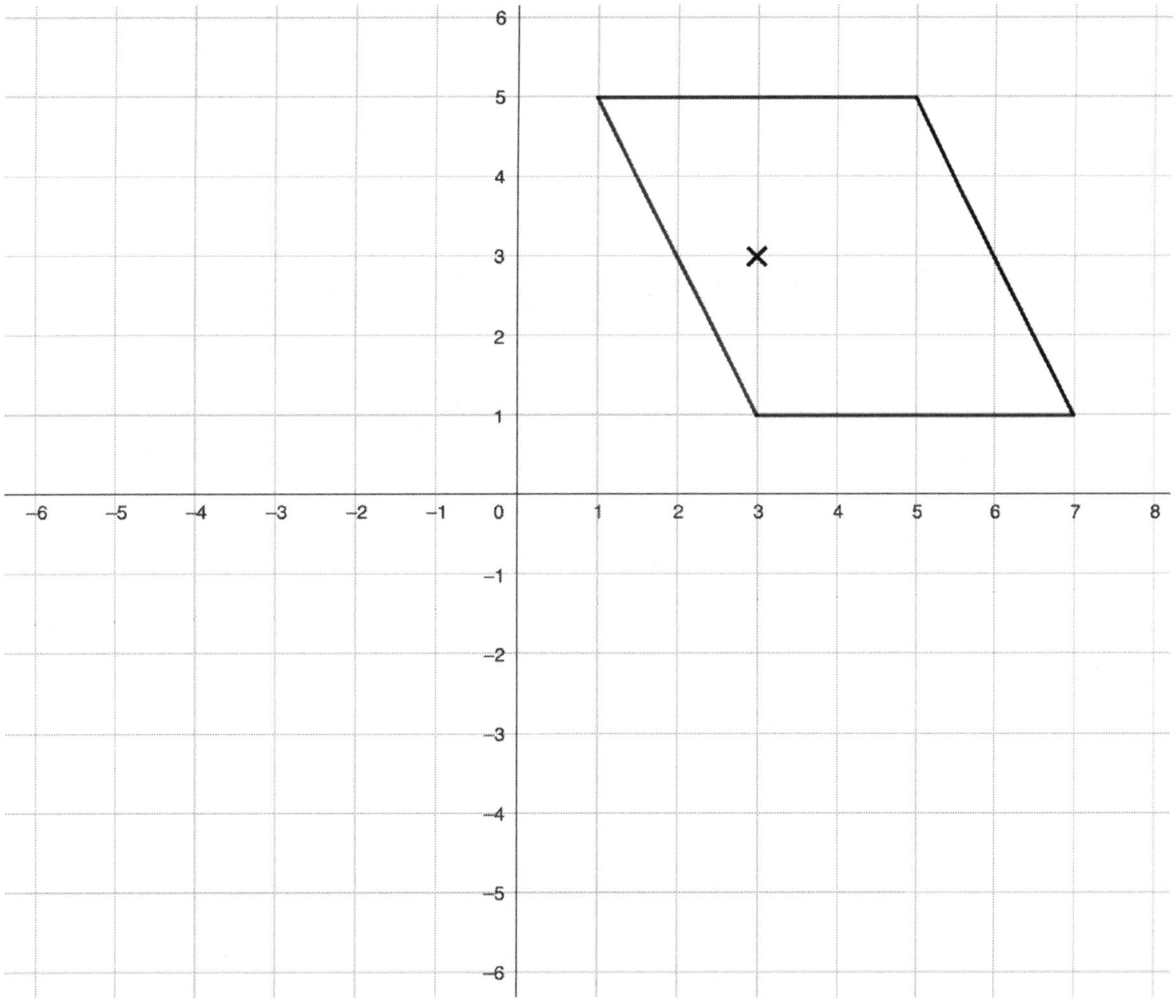

Enlarge the rhombus by a scale factor of -0.5 around the point $(3, 3)$.

(Total for Question 8 is 2 marks)

9.

a) Draw the graph $y = x^3 - 2x^2 - x + 3$ for $-3 \leq x \leq 4$.

(4)

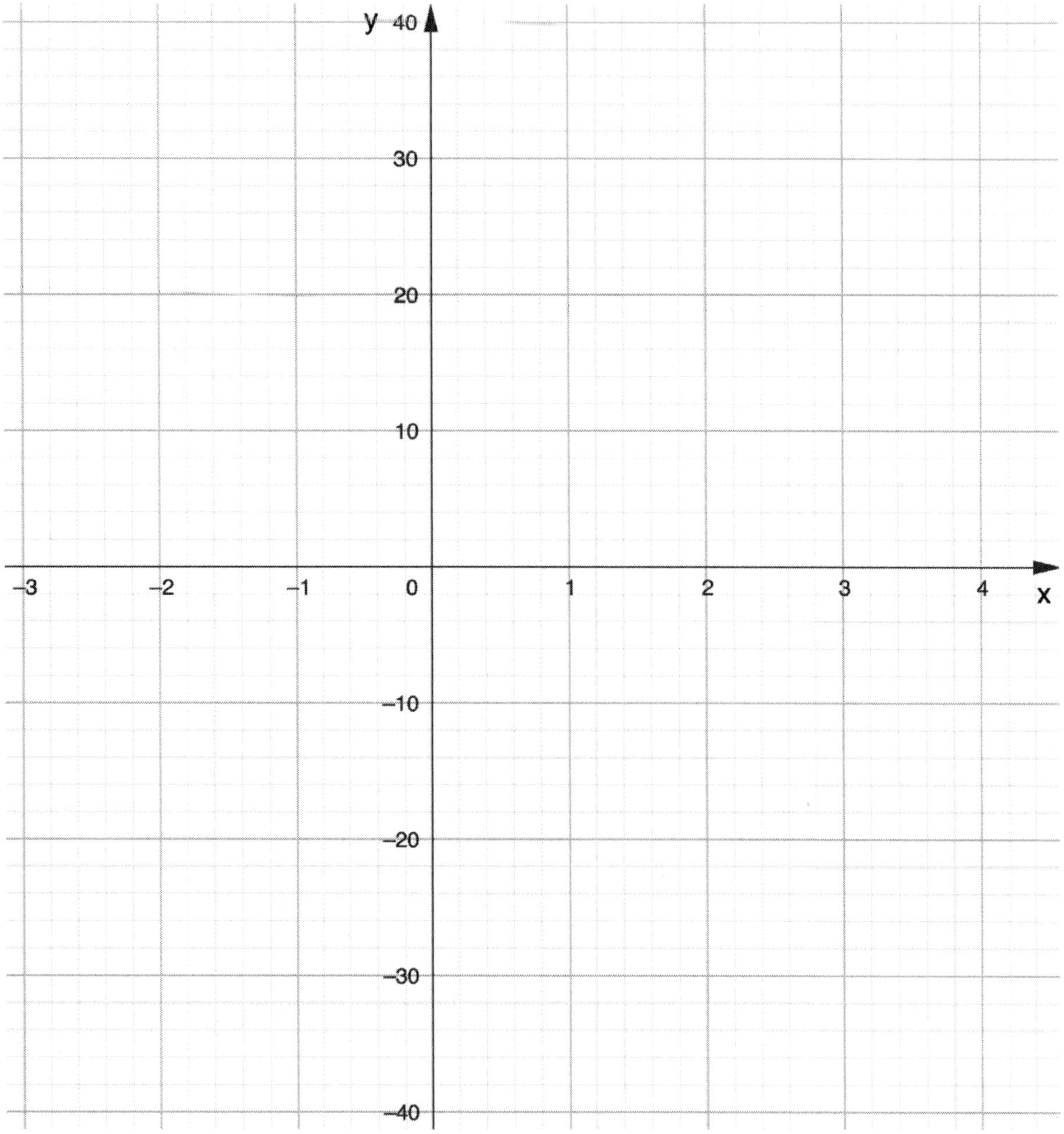

b) Use your graph to estimate the roots of $x^3 - x = 2x^2 + 3$.

....

(2)

(Total for Question 9 is 6 marks)

10. Lara is playing a friendly football match. The probability she wins the match is 0.7.

If Lara wins, the probability she then goes to her favourite restaurant after the match is 0.2.

If Lara does not win, the probability she goes to her favourite restaurant is 0.1.

a) Draw a tree diagram to represent this situation.

(2)

b) Work out the probability she does not go to her favourite restaurant.

....

(2)

(Total for Question 10 is 4 marks)

11. A drinks company are releasing a new water bottle that is similar to their current standard bottle but can carry 20% more water.

The height of the standard bottle is 12.5 cm.

Calculate the height of the new bottle.

Give your answer correct to 3 significant figures.

....

(Total for Question 11 is 4 marks)

12. 40 students were asked if they prefer cheese, olives or ham.

9 of the male students preferred ham.

7 out of the 12 students that preferred olives were female.

10% of the 10 students who preferred cheese were male.

A female student is chosen at random. What is the probability they prefer ham?

....

(Total for Question 12 is 4 marks)

13.

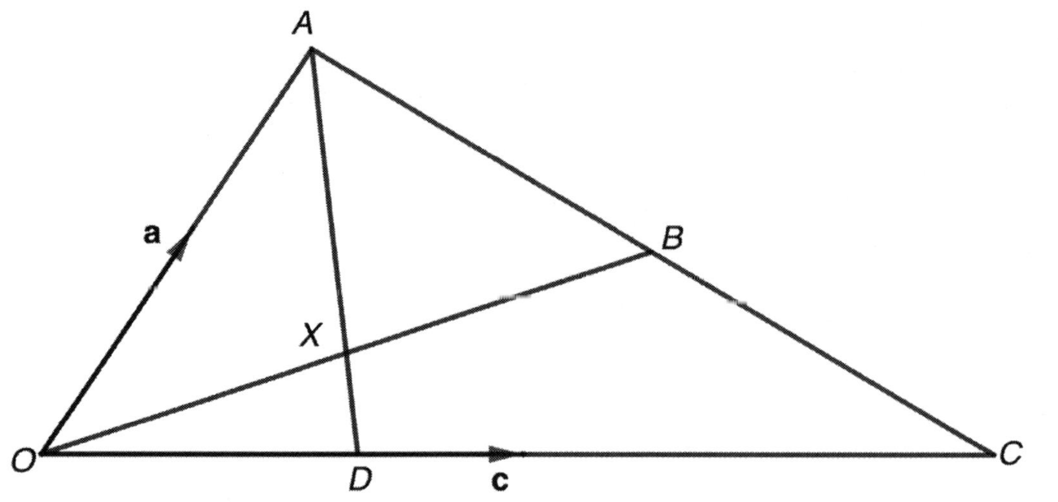

$\overrightarrow{OA} = \mathbf{a}$
$\overrightarrow{OC} = \mathbf{c}$

B is the midpoint of *AC*.
X is the midpoint of *OB*.

a) Find $\overrightarrow{OB}$ in terms of **a** and **c**.

....
(1)

b) Find $\overrightarrow{AX}$ in terms of **a** and **c**.

....
(2)

c) Find $\overrightarrow{AD}$ in terms of **a** and **c**.

....
(3)

(Total for Question 13 is 6 marks)

14.

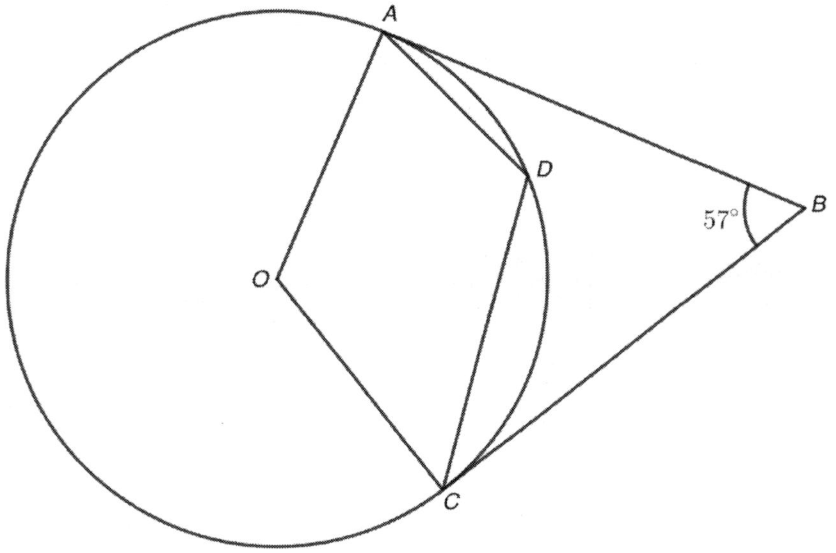

A, D and C are points on the circumference of a circle with centre O.

AB and CB are tangents to the circle.

Angle ABC is 57°.

a) Find angle ADC.
You must give a reason for each stage of your working.

....

(5)

Angle ABC is increased.

b) Without calculation, explain how this would affect your answer to part (a).

....

....

....

(1)

(Total for Question 14 is 6 marks)

15. The histogram shows information about the heights of a sample of bamboo plants.

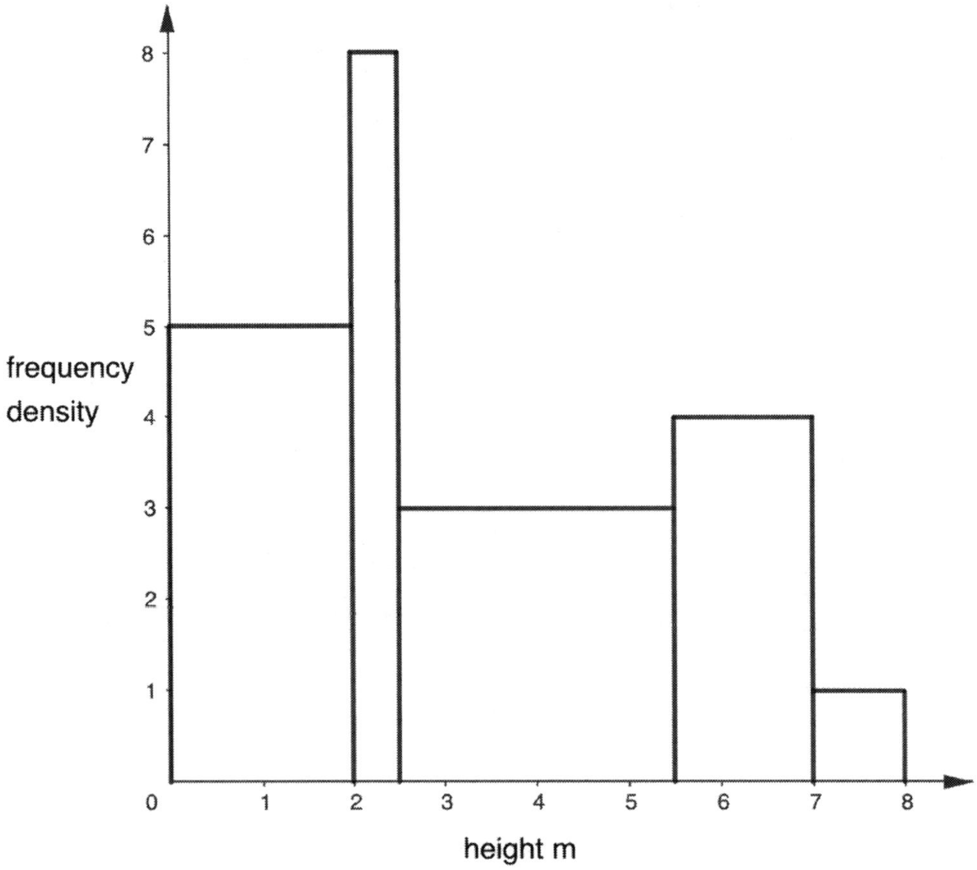

a) Complete the frequency table.

height, h m	frequency
$0 < h \leq 2$	
$2 < h \leq 2.5$	
$2.5 < h \leq 5.5$	
$5.5 < h \leq 7$	
$7 < h \leq 8$	

(2)

b) Estimate the percentage of plants with a height greater than 4.5 m.

....

(2)

(Total for Question 15 is 4 marks)

16. A playground can be modelled as the shape of a rectangle.

The playground has a width 50.27 m to the nearest hundredth.
The playground has a height of 34.8 m to the nearest decimal place.

A student runs 3 laps of the playground.

It takes the student 152.10 seconds to the nearest hundredth.

Find the average speed of the student to 1 decimal place.

....

(Total for Question 16 is 5 marks)

17.

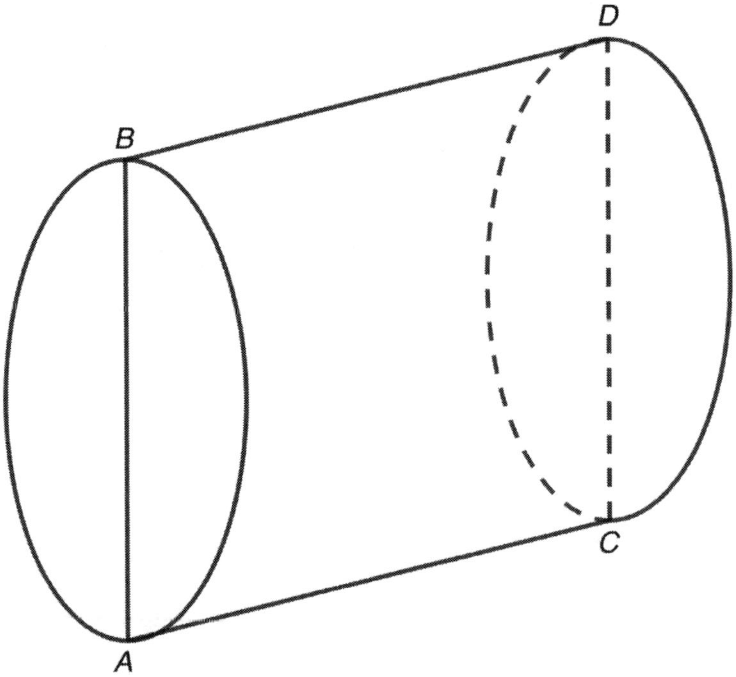

The diagram shows a cylinder.

AB is the vertical diameter of the circle at one end of the cylinder.
CD is the vertical diameter of the circle at the other end of the cylinder.

The radius of each circle is 5 cm and the volume of the cylinder is 200 cm^3.

Find the length *AD*.
Give your answer correct to 3 significant figures.

....

(Total for Question 17 is 5 marks)

18.

a) Show the equation $x^3 + 4x = 4x^2 + 1$ can be rearranged to $x = \sqrt{4x - 4 + \frac{1}{x}}$

(2)

b) Starting with $x_0 = 6$ use the iteration formula $x_{n+1} = \sqrt{4x_n + \frac{1}{x_n} - 4}$ three times to find an estimate for a root to $x^3 + 4x = 4x^2 + 1$.

....

(2)

(Total for Question 18 is 4 marks)

TOTAL FOR PAPER IS 80 MARKS

WRITE INSIDE THE
GREY BORDER

Surname	
Other Names	
Signature	

Centre Number	
Candidate Number	

The Exam Library

Edexcel Mathematics Higher Platinum Tier

GCSE (9-1)

Paper 3 (Calculator)

Total

1 hour 30 minutes

You may use a calculator for this paper.

Instructions

- Use black ink or ball-point pen.
- Fill in the boxes at the top of this page with your surname, other names, centre number and candidate number.
- Answer the questions in the spaces provided.
- Show sufficient working to make your methods clear. Answers that do not show full working may not be awarded full marks.
- Answers should be given to three significant figures unless otherwise stated.

Advice

- Read each question carefully.
- Check your answers at the end if you have time.
- Try to answer every question.

Information

- There are 18 questions in this paper. The total number of marks for this paper is 80.
- The marks for each question are shown in brackets.
- Platinum tier papers are designed to be more difficult than a normal higher tier paper exam. This paper comprises questions from grade 5 to “grade 10”.

Write down all of your working for each question.

1.

a) Simplify $\frac{a^{7/2}}{a^{-3/2}}$

....
(1)

b) Simplify $\left(\sqrt{2}a^3b^{1/2}\right)^6$

....
(1)

c) Simplify $\frac{6x^5y^{-7/2}}{20x\sqrt{xy}}$

....
(2)

(Total for Question 1 is 4 marks)

2. The scatter diagram shows information about the ages of 10 boys, in years, and their heights, in centimetres.

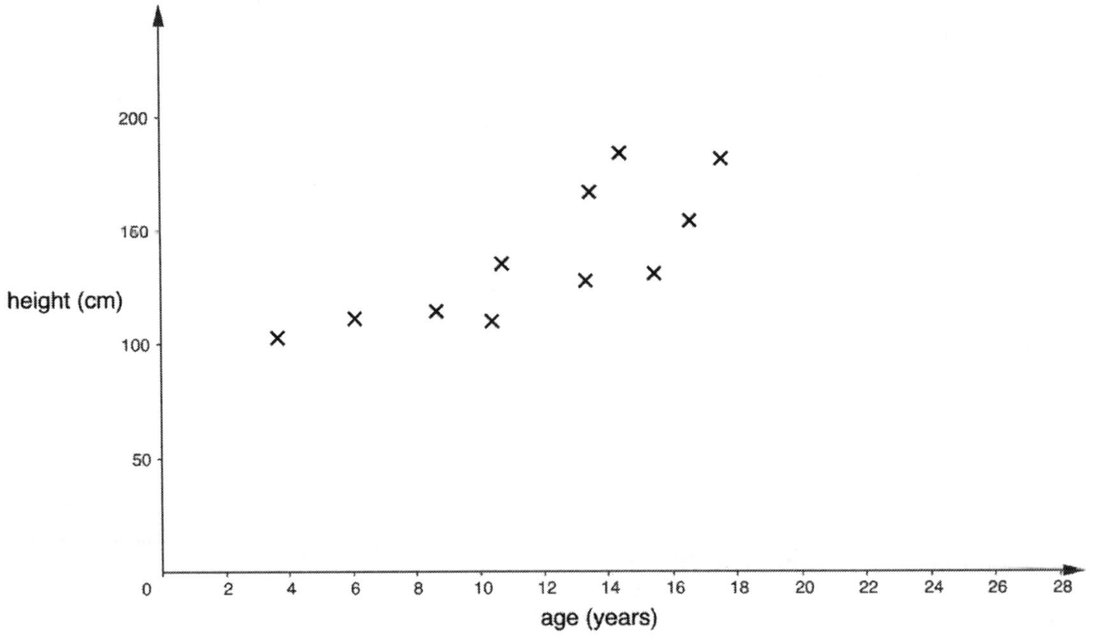

a) Nigel is 9 years old. Use the graph to estimate his height.

....

(1)

b) Explain why the graph is not useful to estimate the height of a 28 year old.

(1)

(Total for Question 2 is 2 marks)

3. A gas is stored in a container the shape of a cube.

The mass of the gas is increased by 30%.

The length of one side of the cube is increased by 10%.

Find the percentage change of the density of the gas inside the cube, if there is any at all.

....

(Total for Question 3 is 4 marks)

4.

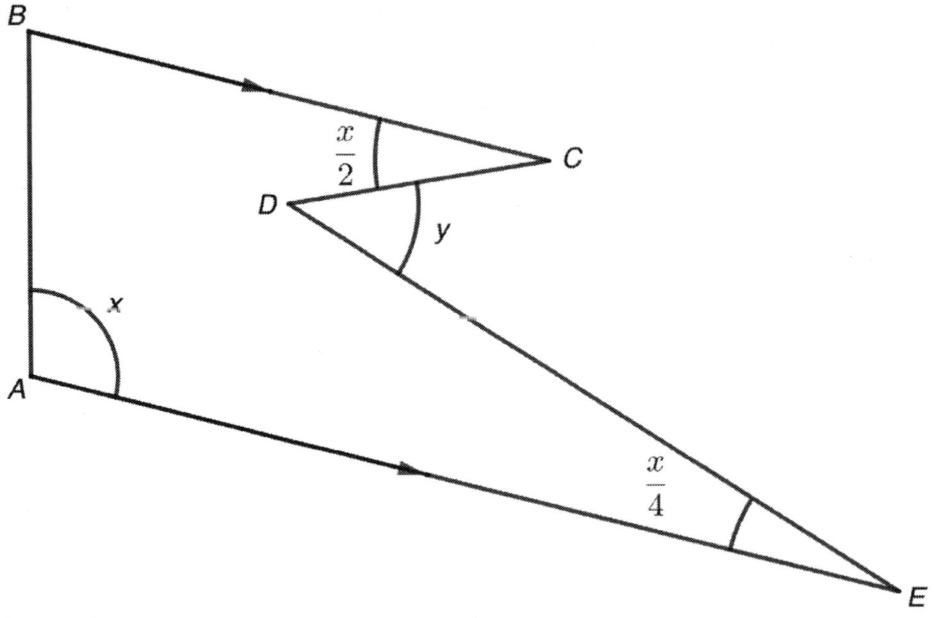

ABCDE is a pentagon.

BC and *AE* are parallel.

Angle $BAE = x$

Angle $BCD = \frac{x}{2}$

Angle $AED = \frac{x}{4}$

Angle $CDE = y = \frac{x}{10} + 39$

Calculate the size of the angle *y*.

....

(Total for Question 4 is 5 marks)

5. Solve the equation $x + 1 = \frac{10 - x}{x}$

Give your answers exactly.

....

(Total for Question 5 is 4 marks)

6. In a street of 43 houses,

23 houses have red roses in the front garden,
25 houses have white roses in the front garden and
10 houses have neither whites roses, nor red roses in the front garden.

Given a house has red roses in the front garden, find the probability it also has white roses in the front garden.

....

(Total for Question 6 is 4 marks)

7.

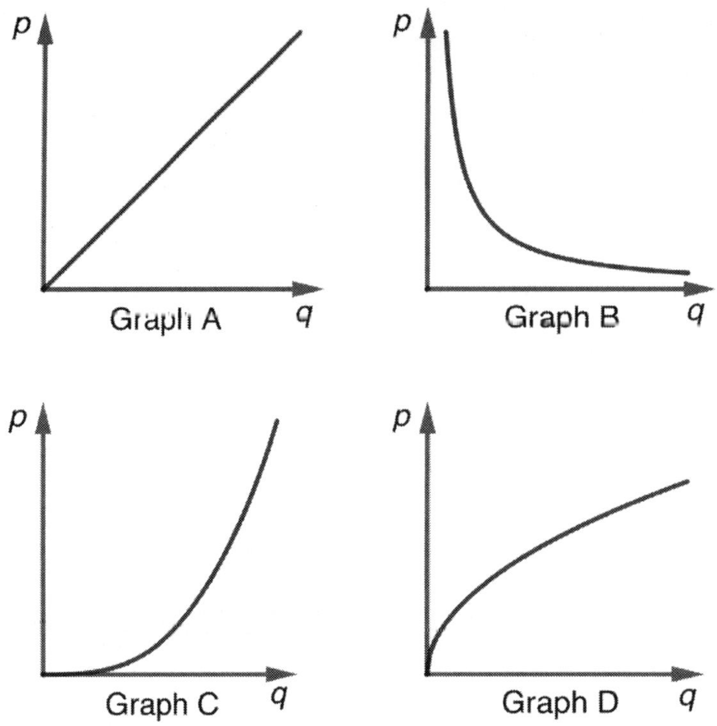

The graphs of p against q represent 4 different types of proportionality. Match each type of proportionality in the table to the correct graph.

Type of Proportionality	Graph Letter
$p \propto q$	
$p \propto \sqrt{q}$	
$p \propto \frac{1}{q^2}$	
$p \propto q^3$	

(Total for Question 7 is 2 marks)

8. Ann, Bill and Charlie work in a warehouse.

They each fill a different sized box with as many of the same size toy as will fit in the box.

When they have filled a box, they place it on the back of a truck to be delivered.

Ann packs 16 toys into her type of box before it is loaded onto the back of the truck.
Bill packs 32 toys into his type of box before it is loaded onto the back of the truck.
Charlie packs 40 toys into his type of box before it is loaded onto the back of the truck.

a) How many boxes will Bill have packed when they all load onto the back of the truck at the same time?

You may assume the time to load a box on the back of a truck is negligible, all 3 people pack the toys at the same rate and they start packing at the same time.

....

(3)

b) Ann now packs twice as slow as the other two. Explain why this does not affect your answer to part (a).

....

....

....

(1)

(Total for Question 8 is 4 marks)

9. A model house is mathematically similar to an actual house.

The ratio of the volumes is 3: 7000

Given the surface area of the model house is 5.2 m^2, find the surface area of the actual house.

Give your answer correct to 3 significant figures.

....

(Total for Question 9 is 4 marks)

10.

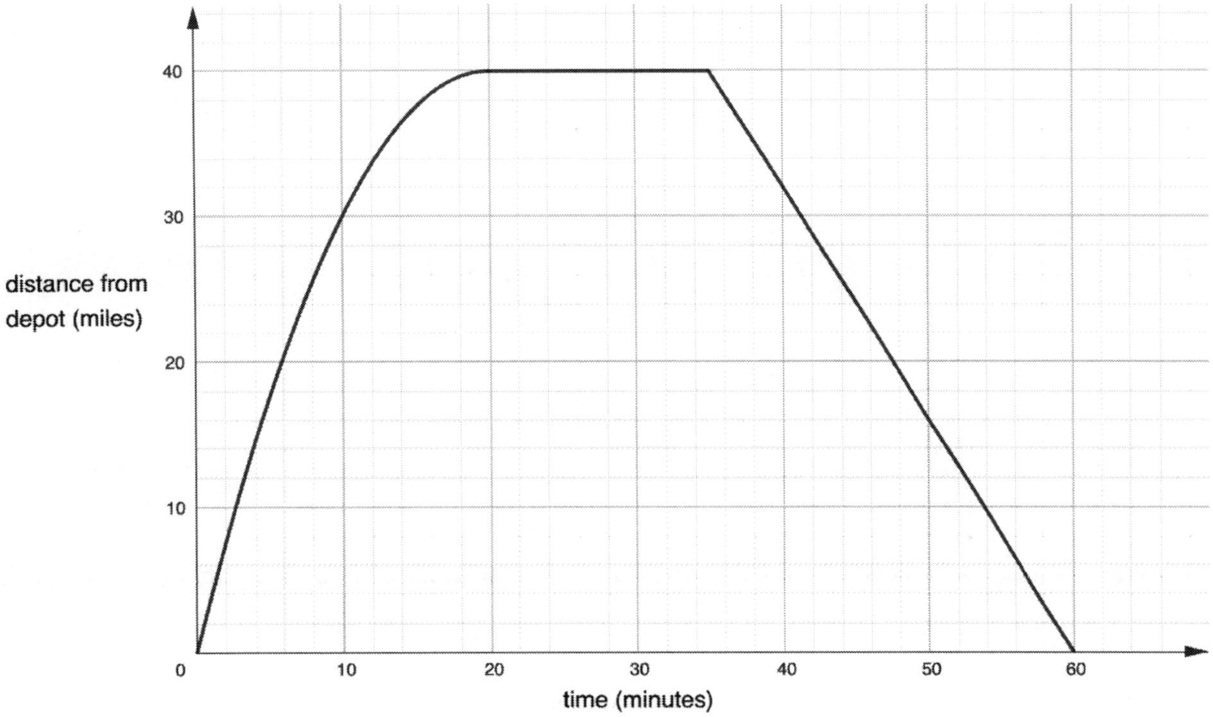

The graph shows the motion of a lorry travelling along a straight road after it has left a depot.

a) Use the graph the estimate the speed of the lorry 15 minutes after it started its journey. Give your answer in miles per hour.

....
(2)

b) Find the average speed of the lorry in the first 35 minutes.

....
(2)

Sally claims

"The lorry is accelerating in the first 20 minutes of motion."

c) Is Sally correct? Give a reason to support your answer.

(1)

(Total for Question 10 is 5 marks)

11. The third and seventh term in a geometric progression are 16 and 4 respectively.

a) Find the first term.

....

(2)

The third, fourth, fifth, sixth and seventh terms of a quadratic sequence are

10, 12, 16, 22, 30

b) State the first two terms.

....

(2)

c) Find an expression, in terms of n, for the nth term.

....

(3)

(Total for Question 11 is 7 marks)

12.

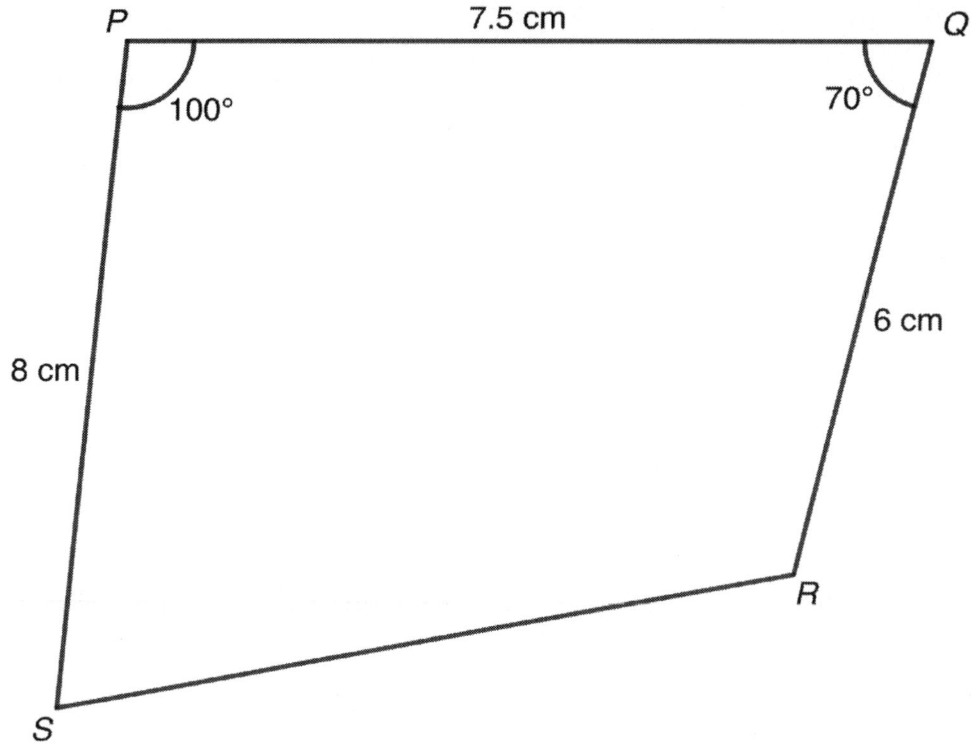

PQRS is a quadrilateral.

Angle $SPQ = 100°$
Angle $PQR = 70°$

$SP = 8$ cm
$PQ = 7.5$ cm
$QR = 6$ cm

Find the size of angle *PSR*.

....

(Total for Question 12 is 5 marks)

13. A biased 4-sided dice is numbered 1 to 4.

The probability of getting a 1 is twice as much as a 4. The probability of a 2 is a third of the probability of getting a 3.

The random variable X represents the number the dice lands on.

a) Complete the table.

x	1	2	3	4
$P(X = x)$			$\frac{1}{2}$	

....

(2)

The biased dice is rolled and the score is recorded.

Afterwards a fair 4-sided dice is rolled and the score is recorded.

b) Work out the probability the sum of the scores on the die is 5.

....

(4)

(Total for Question 13 is 6 marks)

14.

9	4	3	7	2

The diagram shows 5 cards, each with a different number on.

Matt places the cards in different orders to make a 5-digit number. For example, 43927 is a number he can make.

a) Work out how many distinct 5-digit numbers he can make using the cards.

....
(2)

9	4	3	7	2	3

An extra card is added.

b) Work out how many distinct 6-digit numbers he can make with the 6 cards.

....
(3)

(Total for Question 14 is 5 marks)

15.

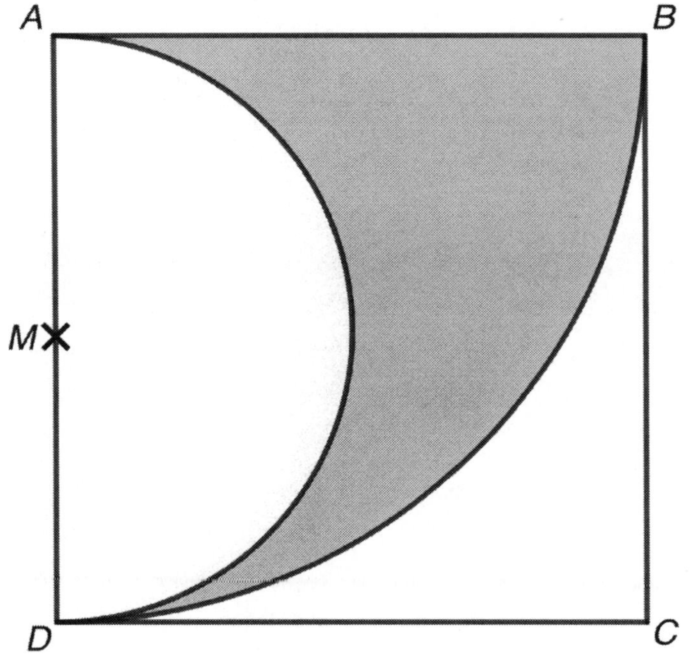

ABCD is a square.

The arc *AD* is a part of a circle with centre *M*.
The arc *BD* is part of a circle with centre *A*.

Find the percentage of the circle that is shaded.
Give you answer correct to 3 significant figures.

....

(Total for Question 15 is 5 marks)

16.

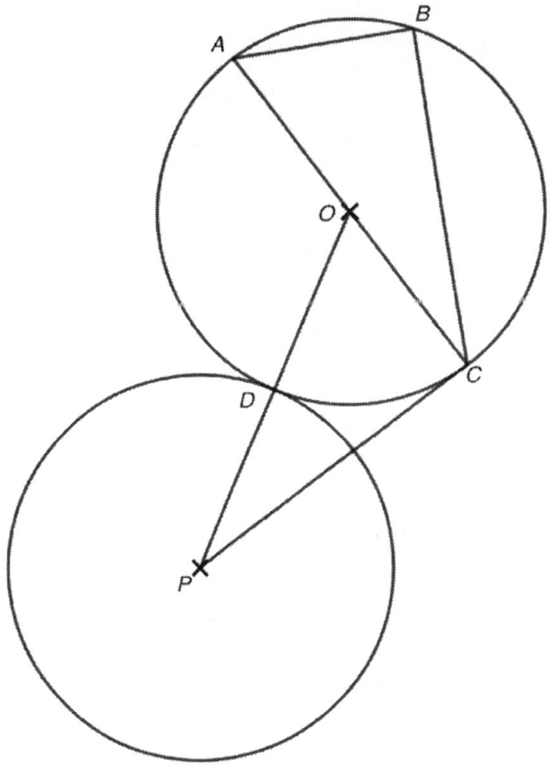

A, B, C and D are points on the circumference of a circle with centre O.

D is also on the circumference of the circle with centre P.

Both circles have the same radius.

CP is a tangent to the circle with centre O.

AB is the length of the radii of the circles.

Prove triangle ABC is congruent to triangle OCP.
You must give a reason for each stage of your working.

(Total for Question 16 is 5 marks)

17.

a) Draw the curve $2x^2 + 2y^2 = 12.5$ on the axes below.

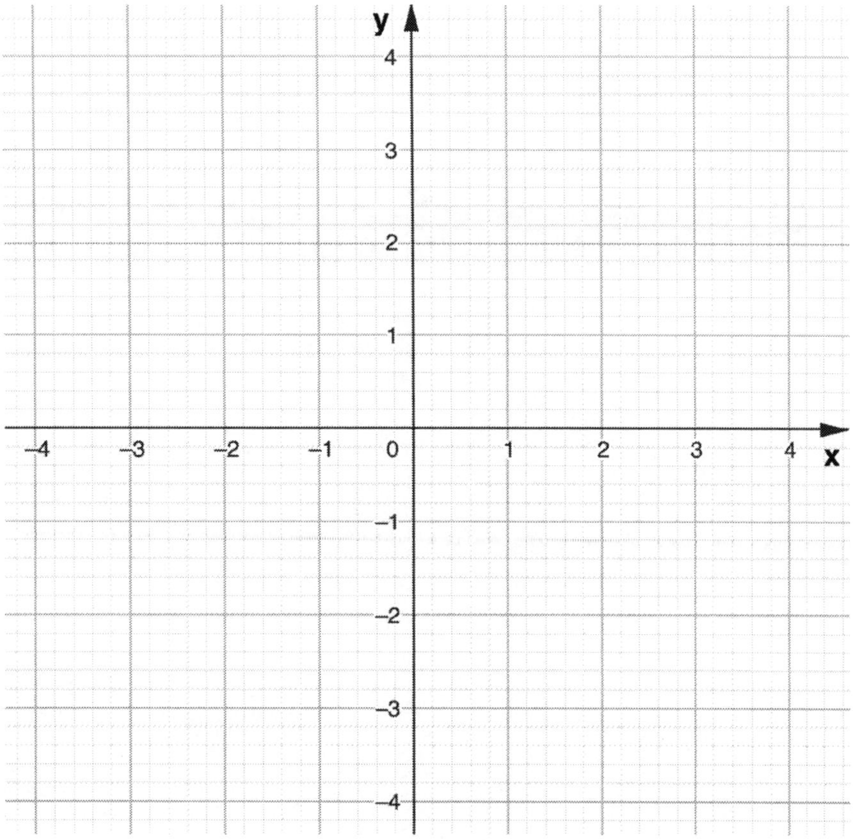

(2)

b) Hence, estimate the solutions to the simultaneous equations

$$2x^2 + 2y^2 = 12.5$$
$$x - y = -1$$

....

(3)

(Total for Question 17 is 5 marks)

18. The curve C is given by the equation $2x^2 + y + 7k^2 = 5kx$ where k is a fixed constant.

Find the coordinates of the maximum point in terms of k.

....

(Total for Question 18 is 4 marks)

TOTAL FOR PAPER IS 80 MARKS

Paper 1

Mark Scheme

Questions	Scheme	Marks
1.	$4.375 = 4\frac{3}{8}$ or $4.375 = \frac{35}{8}$	M1
	$\frac{5}{24} - \frac{35}{8} \rightarrow \frac{5}{24} - \frac{105}{24}$ (finding a common denominator)	M1
	$-\frac{100}{24} \rightarrow -\frac{25}{6}$	A1
		(3)
		3 marks
2.	7, 11, 11, 13 (for at least three of the numbers)	M1
	$11011 = 7 \times 11 \times 11 \times 13$	A1
		(2)
		2 marks
3.	12.5% of £8 = £1 (50% is £4, 25% is £2)	P1
	Total revenue = £8 + £1 = £9 £9 ÷ £1.50 = 6 ∴ 6 boxes were sold	P1
	$15 \times 6 = 90$	A1
		(3)
		3 marks
4.	blue:red = 50:15 and red:yellow 15:24	P1
	$50 + 15 + 24 = 89$ 1 part is worth $44.5 \div 89 = 0.5$ litres	P1
	$0.5 \times 24 = 12$ litres of yellow paint	A1
		(3)

Questions	Scheme	Marks
		3 marks
5. (a)	6.38 tonnes → 6380 kg ≈ 6000 kg OR 489 litres → 0.489 m^3 ≈ 0.5 m^3 OR 55.4 kg/m^3 ≈ 50 kg/m^3	P1
	volume $= \frac{6000}{50} = 120$ m^3	P1
	$\frac{120}{0.5} = 240$ boxes	A1
		(3)
(b)	A greater mass will fit inside a unit volume. Therefore the worker will require fewer boxes.	C1
		(1)
		4 marks
6. (a)	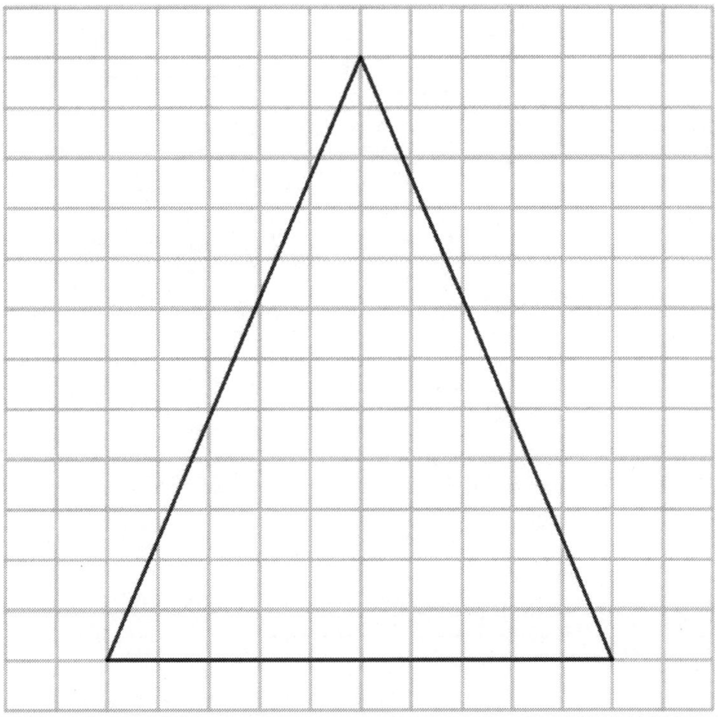	M1A1
		(2)
(b)	$\pi r^2 = \pi \times 5^2 = 25\pi$ OR	

Questions	Scheme	Marks
	$\pi rl = \pi \times 5 \times \sqrt{12^2 + 5^2} = 65\pi$	M1
	$25\pi + 65\pi$	M1
	90π cm^2	A1B1
		(4)
		6 marks
7.	x coordinate of B is $\frac{2+6}{2} = 4$	M1
	Considering the right-angled triangle that forms when a vertical line is drawn downwards from B.	M1
	Using angle BAC as 60°	B1
	height of the triangle is $4 \sin 60 = 2\sqrt{3}$	M1
	B has coordinates $(4, 2 + 2\sqrt{3})$	A1
		(5)
		5 marks
8.	Reflection in the line $x = 3$ OR	B2
	Rotation with centre (3,1), 90° counter clockwise	B2
		(2)
		2 marks
9. (a)	2	B1
		(1)

Questions	Scheme	Marks
(b)	-1	B1
		(1)
(c)	$\frac{1}{27^{5/6}}$	M1
	$=\frac{1}{(27^{1/3})^{5/2}}$	M1
	$=\frac{1}{(3)^{5/2}}=\frac{1}{(3^{1/2})^5}=\frac{1}{9\sqrt{3}}$	M1
	$=\frac{\sqrt{3}}{27}$	A1
		(4)
		6 marks
10. (a)	$\mathrm{g}(0)=\frac{2}{(0+2)^2}=\frac{1}{2}$	M1
	$\mathrm{f}\left(\frac{1}{2}\right)=\left(\frac{1}{2}-2\right)^2=\frac{9}{4}$	A1
		(2)
(b)	$\mathrm{f}(\mathrm{g}(x)=\left(\frac{2}{(x+2)^2}-2\right)^2$	M1
	$=\left(\frac{2}{(x+2)^2}-\frac{2(x+2)^2}{(x+2)^2}\right)^2=\left(\frac{-2x^2-8x-6}{(x+2)^2}\right)^2$	M1
	$=\left(\frac{-2(x^2+4x+3)}{(x+2)^2}\right)^2=\left(\frac{-2(x+1)(x+3)}{(x+2)^2}\right)^2$	M1
	$=\frac{4(x+1)^2(x+3)^2}{(x+2)^4}$	A1
		(4)
		6 marks
11.	Angle $ABC=90°$ (angles formed in a semi-circle are 90°)	M1C1

Questions	Scheme	Marks
	Angle $DBC = 90°$ (angles on a straight line around the same point sum to 180°)	M1C1
	Angle $BDC = (90 - x)°$ (angles in a triangle sum to 180°)	A1
		(5)
		5 marks
12.	$e = \dfrac{k}{f^n}$	B1
	$8 = \dfrac{k}{1^n}$ OR $0.5 = \dfrac{k}{2^n}$	M1
	$8 = \dfrac{k}{1^n} \Rightarrow k = 8 \times 1^n = 8$	M1
	$0.5 = \dfrac{8}{2^n} \Rightarrow 2^n = 16 \Rightarrow n = 4$	M1
	$e = \dfrac{8}{f^4}$	A1
		(5)
		5 marks
13.	$\dfrac{9x^2 + 12x}{9x^2 + 6x - 8} - \dfrac{6x + 4}{9x^2 - 4} \equiv \dfrac{3x(3x + 4)}{(3x - 2)(3x + 4)} - \dfrac{2(3x + 2)}{(3x + 2)(3x - 2)}$	M1
	$\equiv \dfrac{3x}{(3x - 2)} - \dfrac{2}{(3x - 2)}$	M1
	$\equiv \dfrac{3x - 2}{(3x - 2)}$	M1
	$\equiv 1 \equiv a$	A1
		(4)
		4 marks
14.	Uses $\sin 60 = \dfrac{\sqrt{3}}{2}$ OR $\sin 45 = \dfrac{\sqrt{2}}{2}$	B1

Questions	Scheme	Marks
	Attempts to use the sine rule	M1
	$\frac{BC}{\sin 60} = \frac{\sqrt{18}}{\sin 45}$	M1
	$BC = \frac{\sqrt{18}}{\sin 45} \times \sin 60 = \frac{\sqrt{18}}{\sqrt{2}/_2} \times \frac{\sqrt{3}}{2} = \frac{\sqrt{18}}{1} \times \frac{2}{\sqrt{2}} \times \frac{\sqrt{3}}{2}$	M1
	$\Rightarrow BC = 3\sqrt{3}$ cm	A1
		(5)
		5 marks
15.	Let n be an integer. Either $n = 3m, n = 3m + 1$ or $n = 3m - 1$	M1
	If $n = 3m$, then $n^2 = (3m)^2 = 9m^2 = 3(3m^2)$	M1
	If $n = 3m{+}1$, then $n^2 = (3m + 1)^2 = 9m^2 + 6m + 1$ $= 3(3m^2 + 2m) + 1$	M1
	If $n = 3m - 1$, then $n^2 = (3m - 1)^2 = 9m^2 - 6m + 1$ $= 3(3m^2 - 2m) + 1$	M1
	Therefore, every square number is a multiple of 3 or one more than a multiple of 3.	C1
		(5)
		5 marks
16.	$AB^2 + BC^2 = AC^2$	B1
	$\Rightarrow (x - 5)^2 + (9 - x)^2 + (x - 1)^2 + (x - 5)^2 = 8^2$	M1
	$4x^2 - 40x + 132 = 64$ $\Rightarrow x^2 - 10x + 17 = 0$	M1

Questions	Scheme	Marks
	$x = \frac{-(-10) \pm \sqrt{(-10)^2 - 4 \times 1 \times 17}}{2 \times 1} = 5 \pm 2\sqrt{2}$	M1
	$\Rightarrow A$ is $(3 + 2\sqrt{2}, 5 + 2\sqrt{2})$ OR $(3 - 2\sqrt{2}, 5 - 2\sqrt{2})$	A1
		(5)
		5 marks
17.	There are $3n$ blue counters and $4n$ red counters in the bag.	P1
	Number of red counters after one is removed is $4n - 1$ Number of counters after one is removed is $7n - 1$ The probability Sally removes a second red is $\frac{4n-1}{7n-1} = \frac{5}{9}$	P1
	$36\text{n} - 9 = 35n - 5 \Rightarrow n = 4$	P1
	Therefore, there were originally 12 blue counters	A1
		(4)
		4 marks
18.	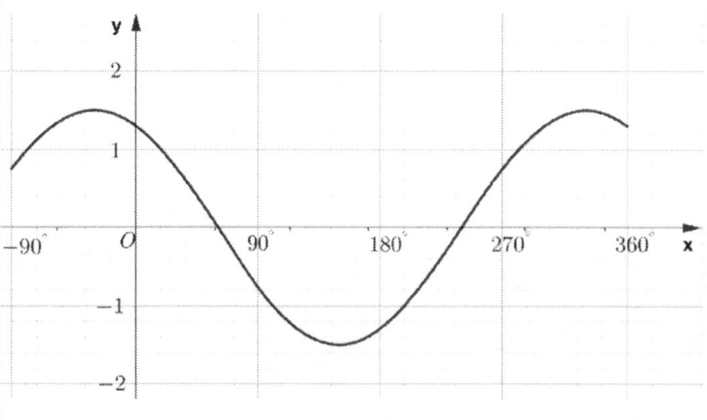 Min and max at 1.5 and -1.5	B1
	Shifted 30 to the left	B1
	Graph is the shape of a wave	B1
		(3)
		3 marks

Questions	Scheme	Marks
19.	$y = \sqrt{3}\left(x^2 + \frac{6}{\sqrt{3}}x\right) + 19$	M1
	$y = \sqrt{3}\left(\left(x + \frac{3}{\sqrt{3}}\right)^2 - 3\right) + 19$	M1
	$y = \sqrt{3}\left(x + \frac{3}{\sqrt{3}}\right)^2 + 19 - 3\sqrt{3}$	M1
	therefore the minimum point is $(-\sqrt{3}, 19 - 3\sqrt{3})$	A1
		(4)
		4 marks

Paper 2

Mark Scheme

Questions	Scheme	Marks
1.	$264 = 2^3 \times 3 \times 11$ OR $4356 = 2^2 \times 3^2 \times 11^2$	M1
	therefore HCF $= 2^2 \times 3 \times 11$	M1
	$= 132$	A1
		(3)
		3 marks
2. (a)	$6a^3 + 6x$	B1
		(1)
(b)	$2x^4 - 4x^2y\sqrt{x} + 16xy\sqrt{x}$	M1A1
		(2)
(c)	$\sqrt{x} + x\sqrt{x} + 10\sqrt{x} = x\sqrt{x} + 11\sqrt{x}$	M1A1
		(2)
		5 marks
3.	Let V be the amount Miguel buys the car for. After 3 years the value is 1.05^3V	P1
	Total profit is $1.05^3V - V$	P1
	Ratio is $V : 1.05^3V - V = 1 : 1.05^3 - 1$	P1
	$1 : 0.157625$	A1
		(4)
		4 marks
4. (a)	$y = \frac{1}{2}x + c$ as it must be perpendicular	M1

Questions	Scheme	Marks
	$y = -2(0) + 5 = 5$ and $y = -2(4) + 5 = -3 \rightarrow (0, 5)$ & $(4, -3)$ $\left(\frac{0+4}{2}, \frac{5+-3}{2}\right) = (2, 1)$ (midpoint of line)	M1
	$1 = \frac{1}{2}(2) + c \Rightarrow c = 0$	M1
	$y = \frac{1}{2}x$	A1
		(4)
(b)	Tries to find two points equidistant from (2, 1) on the line above	M1
	For a correct range eg $-6 \leq x \leq 10$	A1
		(2)
		6 marks
5.	$x^2 - 10x + 24 = 0$	M1
	$(x - 4)(x - 6) = 0$	M1
	$x = 4, 6$	A1
		(3)
		3 marks
6.	uses lower bound of distance 9500 m	P1
	uses upper bound of speed 14.5 kmh^{-1}	P1
	$\text{time} = \frac{\text{distance}}{\text{speed}} = \frac{9.5}{14.5} = 0.655$ hours	P1
	$0.655 \times 60 = 39.3$ minutes	A1
		(4)

Questions	Scheme	Marks
		4 marks
7.	Angle $SPQ = \tan^{-1}\dfrac{10}{6} = 59.0°$	M1
	Angle $PSR = 59.0°$ (alternate angles)	M1C1
	Angle QRS = Angle $TRS = 180 - 90 - 59.0 = 31.0°$ (angles in a triangle sum to 180°)	A1C1
		(5)
		5 marks
8.	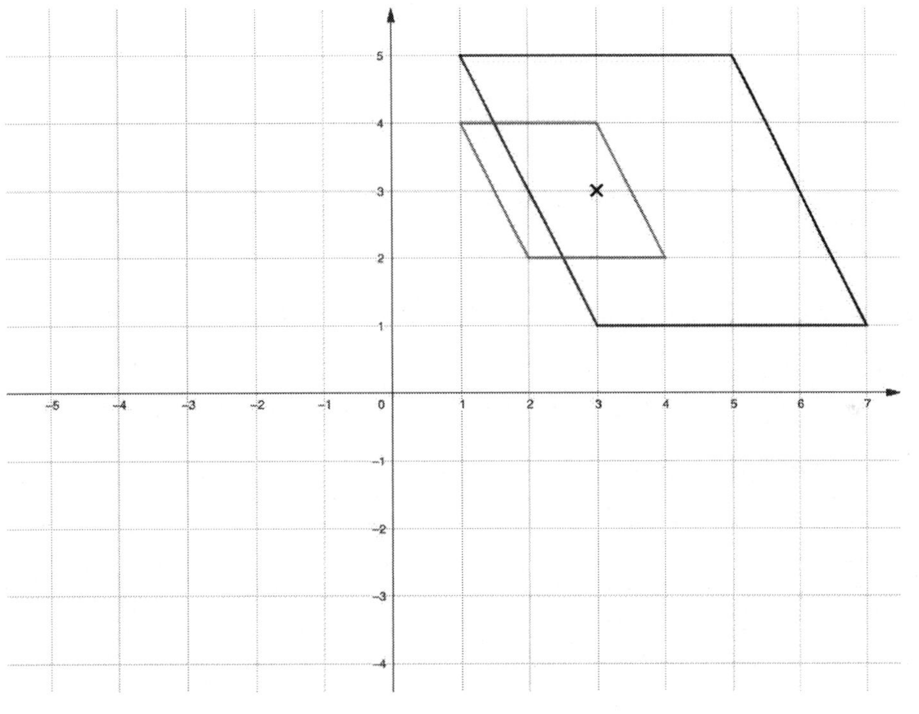	B1 (correct size) B2 (completely correct)
		(2)
		2 marks

Questions	Scheme	Marks
9. (a)	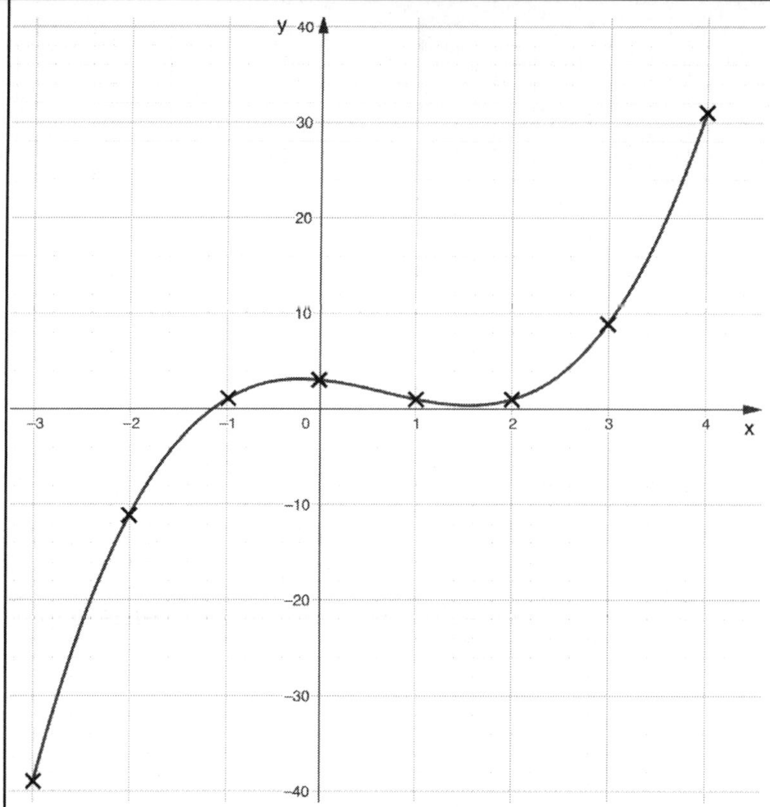	
	Table of values to plot points	M1
	All y values calculated correctly	A1
	Points plotted correctly	A1
	Points joined with a smooth curve	A1
		(4)
(b)	Rearranges equation to get $x^3 - 2x^2 - x + 3 = 6$	M1
	any value in the range $2.6 \leq x \leq 3$	A1
		(2)
		6 marks
10. (a)	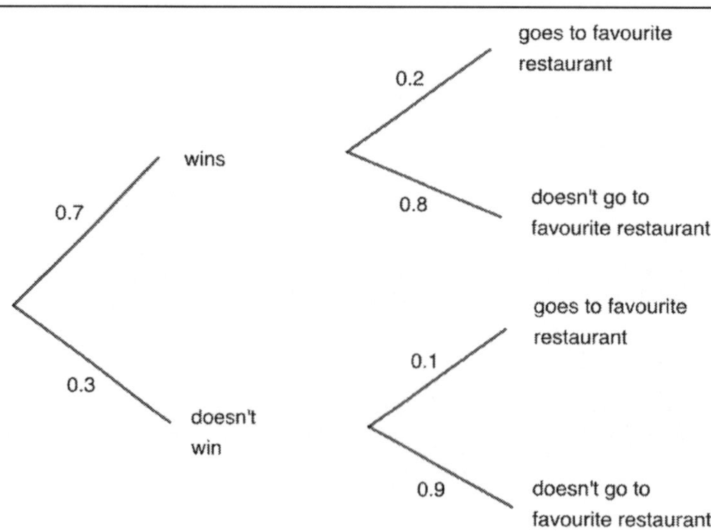	P1A1
		(2)

Questions	Scheme	Marks
(b)	$0.7 \times 0.8 + 0.3 \times 0.9$	P1
	0.83	A1
		(2)
		4 marks
11.	volume scale factor is 1.2	B1
	linear scale factor is $\sqrt[3]{1.2}$	P1
	$\Rightarrow$ new height is $12.5 \times \sqrt[3]{1.2}$	P1
	$\Rightarrow$ new height is 13.3 cm	A1
		(4)
		4 marks
12.	(table below)	B1 (half the entries completed correctly) B1 (fully correct table)
	$\frac{9}{25}$	P1A1
		(4)
		4 marks
13. (a)	$\overrightarrow{OB} = \overrightarrow{OA} + \frac{1}{2}\overrightarrow{AC} = \mathbf{a} + \frac{1}{2}(\mathbf{c} - \mathbf{a}) = \frac{1}{2}\mathbf{a} + \frac{1}{2}\mathbf{c}$	B1
		(1)
(b)	$\overrightarrow{AX} = \overrightarrow{AO} + \overrightarrow{OX} = \overrightarrow{AO} + \frac{1}{2}\overrightarrow{OB}$	M1

Table for question 12:

	Cheese	Olives	Ham	Total
male	1	5	9	15
female	9	7	9	25
total	10	12	18	40

Questions	Scheme	Marks
	$= -\mathbf{a} + \frac{1}{2}\left(\frac{1}{2}\mathbf{a} + \frac{1}{2}\mathbf{c}\right) = -\frac{3}{4}\mathbf{a} + \frac{1}{4}\mathbf{c}$	A1
		(2)
(c)	$\overrightarrow{AD} = \lambda\overrightarrow{AX} = \overrightarrow{AO} + \mu\overrightarrow{OC} \Rightarrow -\frac{3}{4}\lambda\mathbf{a} + \frac{1}{4}\lambda\mathbf{c} = -\mathbf{a} + \mu\mathbf{c}$	M1
	$\Rightarrow \lambda = \frac{4}{3}$	M1
	$\Rightarrow \overrightarrow{AD} = -\mathbf{a} + \frac{1}{3}\mathbf{c}$	A1
		(3)
		6 marks
14. (a)	angle OAB = angle $OCB = 90°$ (tangents meet radii at 90°)	M1
	angle $AOC = 360 - 90 - 90 - 57 = 123°$ (angles in quadrilateral sum to 360°)	M1
	angle $APC = 61.5°$ (angles at the circumference are half the size of angles at the centre when subtended by the same arc) Note: point P is any point on the major arc AC	M1
	angle $ADC = 118.5°$ (opposite angles in a cyclic quadrilateral sum to 180°)	C1A1
		(5)
(b)	If angle ABC increases, angle AOC decreases, which means angle APC decreases. Therefore, angle ADC increases.	C1
		(1)
		6 marks

Questions	Scheme	Marks
15. (a)	<table><tr><th>height, h m</th><th>frequency</th></tr><tr><td>$0 < h \leq 2$</td><td>10</td></tr><tr><td>$2 < h \leq 2.5$</td><td>4</td></tr><tr><td>$2.5 < h \leq 5.5$</td><td>9</td></tr><tr><td>$5.5 < h \leq 7$</td><td>6</td></tr><tr><td>$7 < h \leq 8$</td><td>1</td></tr></table>	M1A1
		(2)
(b)	$\frac{1}{3} \times 9 = 3$ (number of plants between 4.5 cm and 5.5 cm) $\rightarrow \frac{3+6+1}{30} \times 100$	P1
	$= 33.3\%$	A1
		(2)
		4 marks
16.	Lower bound of distance is $(50.265 + 34.75) \times 2 \times 3 = 510.09$ Upper bound of distance $(50.275 + 34.85) \times 2 \times 3 = 510.75$	P1
	Lower bound of time is 152.095 Upper bound of time is 152.105	P1
	Lower bound of speed is $\frac{510.09}{152.105} = 3.353 \ldots$	P1
	Upper bound of speed is $\frac{510.75}{152.095} = 3.3580 \ldots$	P1
	As the lower bound and upper bound round to the same number to 1 decimal place, the average speed is 3.4 ms^{-1}	A1
		(5)
		5 marks

Questions	Scheme	Marks
17.	area of cross section $= \pi \times 5^2 = 25\pi$	P1
	height of cylinder $= \dfrac{200}{25\pi} = \dfrac{8}{\pi}$ cm	P1
	Using the right-angled triangle ACD	P1
	$AD = \sqrt{10^2 + \left(\dfrac{8}{\pi}\right)^2}$	P1
	$AD = 10.3$ cm	A1
		(5)
		5 marks
18. (a)	$x^3 + 4x = 4x^2 + 1 \Rightarrow x^3 = 4x^2 - 4x + 1$ $\Rightarrow x^2 = 4x - 4 + \dfrac{1}{x}$ $\Rightarrow x = \sqrt{4x - 4 + \dfrac{1}{x}}$	M1A1
		(2)
(b)	$x_1 = \sqrt{4(6) - 4 + \dfrac{1}{6}} = 4.4907$	M1
	$x_3 = 3.366158098$	A1
		(2)
		4 marks

Paper 3

Mark Scheme

Questions	Scheme	Marks
1. (a)	a^5	B1
		(1)
(b)	$8a^{18}b^3$	B1
		(1)
(c)	$\dfrac{6x^5y^{-7/2}}{20x^{3/2}y^{1/2}}$	M1
	$\dfrac{3x^{7/2}}{10y^4}$	A1
		(2)
		4 marks
2. (a)	Draws a line of best fit and estimates between 110 cm and 130 cm	B1
		(1)
(b)	The greatest age in the data is 18. Therefore, predicting the height of a 28 year old would be extrapolation- the data might not follow the same pattern at ages greater than 18.	C1
		(1)
		2 marks
3.	Let M be the original mass and V be the original volume. Then the original density is $\dfrac{M}{V}$	B1
	The new mass is $1.3M$, the new volume is 1.1^3V Then the new density is $\dfrac{1.3M}{1.1^3V}$	P1
	new density $= \dfrac{1.3M}{1.1^3V} = \dfrac{1.3}{1.1^3} \times \dfrac{M}{V} = 0.977 \times$ old density	P1
	Therefore there is a 2.3% decrease in density.	A1
		(4)

Questions	Scheme	Marks
		4 marks
4.	Angles in a pentagon sum to $(5-2)\times 180 = 540°$ OR angle $ABC = 180 - x$ (co-interior angles sum to 180°)	M1
	angle $CDE = 360 - \left(\frac{x}{10} + 39\right)$	M1
	$x + (180 - x) + \frac{x}{2} + \left(360 - \left(\frac{x}{10} + 39\right)\right) + \frac{x}{4} = 540$	M1
	$501 + \frac{x}{2} - \frac{x}{10} + \frac{x}{4} = 540$ $\Rightarrow \frac{13x}{20} = 39 \Rightarrow x = 60$	M1
	$\Rightarrow y = 45°$	A1
		(5)
		5 marks
5.	$x^2 + x = 10 - x$	M1
	$x^2 + 2x - 10 = 0$	M1
	$x = \frac{-(2) \pm \sqrt{(2)^2 - 4(1)(-10)}}{2(1)}$	M1
	$x = -1 \pm \sqrt{11}$	A1
		(4)
		4 marks

<table>
<tr><th>Questions</th><th>Scheme</th><th>Marks</th></tr>
<tr><td>6.</td><td>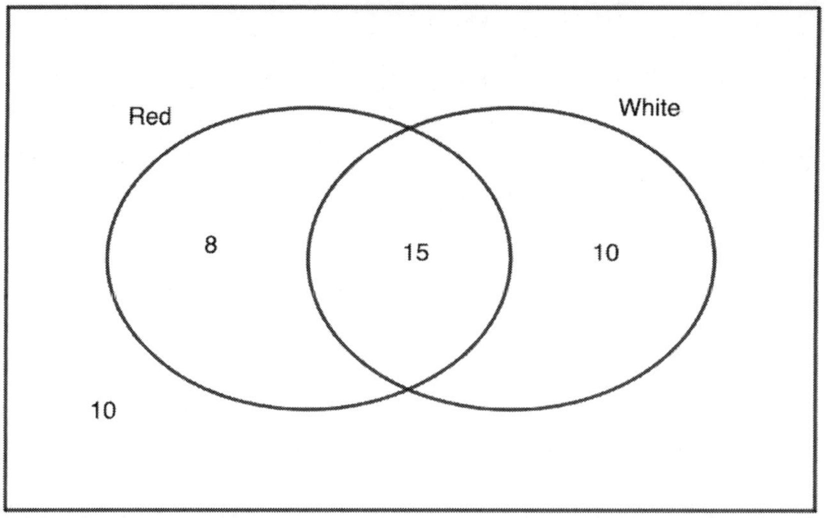
</td><td>P1P1</td></tr>
<tr><td></td><td>$\frac{15}{23}$</td><td>P1A1</td></tr>
<tr><td></td><td></td><td>(4)</td></tr>
<tr><td colspan="3">4 marks</td></tr>
<tr><td>7.</td><td><table>
<tr><th>Type of Proportionality</th><th>Graph Letter</th></tr>
<tr><td>$p \propto q$</td><td>A</td></tr>
<tr><td>$p \propto \sqrt{q}$</td><td>D</td></tr>
<tr><td>$p \propto \frac{1}{q^2}$</td><td>B</td></tr>
<tr><td>$p \propto q^3$</td><td>C</td></tr>
</table></td><td>B1
(at least 2 correct)

B1
(all correct)</td></tr>
<tr><td></td><td></td><td>(2)</td></tr>
<tr><td colspan="3">2 marks</td></tr>
<tr><td>8. (a)</td><td>$16 = 2^4, 32 = 2^5, 40 = 2^3 \times 5$</td><td>P1</td></tr>
<tr><td></td><td>lowest common multiple $= 2^5 \times 5$</td><td>P1</td></tr>
</table>

Questions	Scheme	Marks
	160	A1
		(3)
(b)	If Ann packs twice as slow, she will fill a box with 16 toys in the same time as Bill pack 32 toys into a box. Therefore, they will load the truck at the same times.	C1
		(1)
		4 marks
9.	volume scale factor $= \frac{7000}{3}$	P1
	linear scale factor $= \sqrt[3]{\frac{7000}{3}}$ area scale factor $= \left(\sqrt[3]{\frac{7000}{3}}\right)^2$	P1
	surface area $= 5.2 \times \left(\sqrt[3]{\frac{7000}{3}}\right)^2$	P1
	$= 915\text{ m}^2$	A1
		(4)
		4 marks
10. (a)	Drawing a tangent at 15 minutes and attempting to find the gradient	P1
	Gradient is approximately 1, therefore the speed is approximately 60 mph	A1
		(2)
(b)	$\frac{40-0}{35} \times 60$	P1

Questions	Scheme	Marks
	68.6 mph	A1
		(2)
(c)	Sally is incorrect. The gradient is decreasing which means the speed is decreasing.	C1
		(1)
		5 marks
11. (a)	$16 \times r^4 = 4 \Rightarrow r = \frac{1}{\sqrt{2}}$	M1
	Therefore the first term is 32	A1
		(2)
(b)	12, 10	B1B1
		(2)
(c)	n^{th} term for a quadratic sequence is $an^2 + bn + c$ The second difference is 2, therefore $a = 1$	M1
	$(1)^2 + 1b + c = 12 \Longrightarrow b + c = 11$ $(2)^2 + 2b + c = 10 \Longrightarrow 2b + c = 6$ therefore $b = -5, \quad c = 16$	M1
	n^{th} term is $n^2 - 5n + 16$	A1
		(3)
		7 marks
12.	$SQ^2 = 8^2 + 7.5^2 - 2 \times 8 \times 7.5 \cos 100 \Longrightarrow SQ = 11.9$ cm	M1
	$\frac{\sin \angle PSQ}{7.5} = \frac{\sin 100}{11.9} \Longrightarrow \angle PSQ = 38.4°$	M1

Questions	Scheme	Marks
	$\Rightarrow \angle PQS = 180 - 100 - 38.4 = 41.6°$ $\Rightarrow \angle SQR = 70 - 41.6 = 28.4°$ $SR^2 = 11.9^2 + 6^2 - 2 \times 11.9 \times 6 \cos 28.4 \Longrightarrow SR = 7.19$ cm	M1
	$\frac{\sin \angle QSR}{6} = \frac{\sin 28.4}{7.19} \Longrightarrow \angle QSR = 23.4°$	M1
	$38.4 + 23.4 = 61.9°$	A1
		(5)
		5 marks
13. (a)	<table><tr><td>x</td><td>1</td><td>2</td><td>3</td><td>4</td></tr><tr><td>$\mathrm{P}(X = x)$</td><td>$\frac{2}{9}$</td><td>$\frac{1}{6}$</td><td>$\frac{1}{2}$</td><td>$\frac{1}{9}$</td></tr></table>	B1 (at least 2 correct) B1 (all correct)
		(2)
(b)	Lists possible options: 1st is 1 and 2nd is 4 1st is 4 and 2nd is 1 1st is 2 and 2nd is 3 1st is 3 and 2nd is 2	P1
	Obtains probabilities $\frac{2}{9} \times \frac{1}{4} = \frac{2}{36}$ $\frac{1}{9} \times \frac{1}{4} = \frac{1}{36}$ $\frac{1}{6} \times \frac{1}{4} = \frac{1}{24}$ $\frac{1}{2} \times \frac{1}{4} = \frac{1}{8}$	P1
	$\frac{2}{36} + \frac{1}{36} + \frac{1}{24} + \frac{1}{8}$	P1

Questions	Scheme	Marks
	$= \frac{1}{4}$	A1
		(4)
		6 marks
14. (a)	$5 \times 4 \times 3 \times 2 \times 1$	M1
	$= 120$	A1
		(2)
(b)	$\frac{6 \times 5 \times 4 \times 3 \times 2 \times 1}{2}$	M1M1
	$= 360$	A1
		(3)
		5 marks
15.	Let the length of one side of the square be $2r$. Area of semi circle $= \frac{\pi r^2}{2}$ OR area of quadrant $= \frac{\pi(2r)^2}{4} = \pi r^2$	M1
	Area of semi circle $= \frac{\pi r^2}{2}$ AND area of quadrant $= \frac{\pi(2r)^2}{4} = \pi r^2$	M1
	area of shaded region $= \pi r^2 - \frac{\pi r^2}{2} = 0.5\pi r^2$	M1
	area of square $= 4r^2$ % of square shaded $= \frac{0.5\pi r^2}{4r^2} \times 100 = \frac{0.5\pi}{4} \times 100$	M1

Questions	Scheme	Marks
	$= 39.3\%$	A1
		(5)
		5 marks
16.	$\angle ABC = 90°$ (angles formed in a semi circle are 90°)	B1
	$\angle OCP = 90°$ (tangents meet the radius at 90°)	B1
	Let r be the radius of circle with centre O. $AC = 2r$ (by definition) $OP = 2r$ (as the circles share the same radius)	M1
	$AB = OC = r$ (by definition)	M1
	Therefore triangles ABC and OCP are congruent as they both have a right angle, a side the same length and a hypotenuse the same length.	C1
		(5)
		5 marks
17. (a)	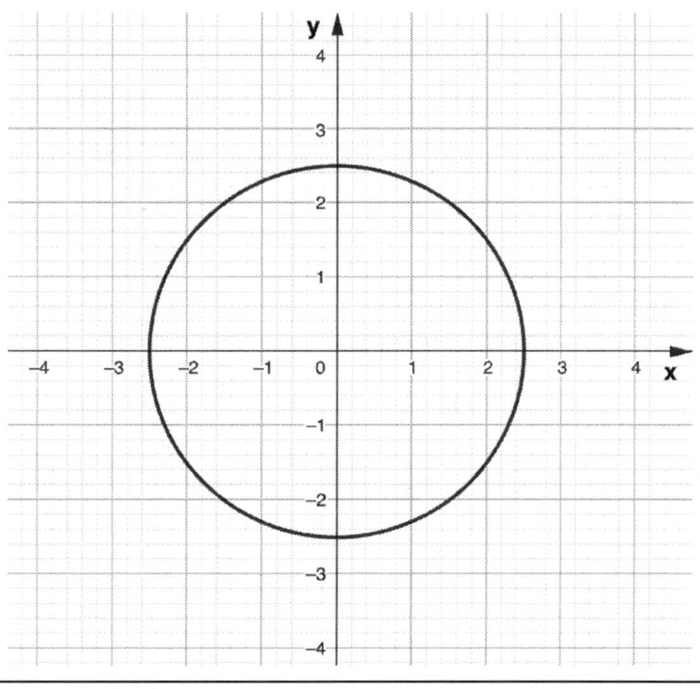	B1 (drawing a circle) B1 (circle with correct centre and radius)
		(2)

Questions	Scheme	Marks
(b)	Draws line $y = x + 1$ on circle	M1
	$x = 1.2, y = 2.2$ OR $x = -2.2, y = -1.2$ (within 0.2 or answers)	A1
	$x = 1.2, y = 2.2$ AND $x = -2.2, y = -1.2$ (within 0.2 or answers)	A1
		(3)
		5 marks
18.	$y = -2x^2 + 5kx - 7k^2$ $y = -2\left(x^2 - \frac{5k}{2}x\right) - 7k^2$	M1
	$y = -2\left(\left(x - \frac{5k}{4}\right)^2 - \frac{25k^2}{16}\right) - 7k^2$	M1
	$y = -2\left(x - \frac{5k}{4}\right)^2 + \frac{25k^2}{8} - 7k^2$	M1
	Therefore the maximum point is $\left(\frac{5k}{4}, -\frac{31k^2}{8}\right)$	A1
		(4)
		4 marks

Printed in Great Britain
by Amazon

23860653R00048